COLLECTIONS

A Harcourt Reading / Language Arts Program

PHONICS PRACTICE READERS

Harcourt

Orlando Boston Dallas Chicago San Diego

Visit *The Learning Site!*
www.harcourtschool.com

3 4 5 6 7 8 9 10 026 2002 01

ISBN 0-15-319818-4

CONTENTS

Happy Chick

by Linda Clifford

Illustrations by Patricia Murphy

Finch and Robin saw an egg on the porch. Chip, chip, crack! Hatch!

"I'm out!" said Happy Chick.
"Let's play ball!" said Finch.

7

Happy Chick couldn't catch.
He ran into a branch and fell.

8

Happy Chick couldn't pitch.
The ball landed in a ditch.

9

Happy Chick was so sad.
"I can't catch or pitch," he said.

"Let's sit and chat," said Finch.
"I can do that!" Happy Chick said.

11

"When it comes to chatting, I'm the champ!"

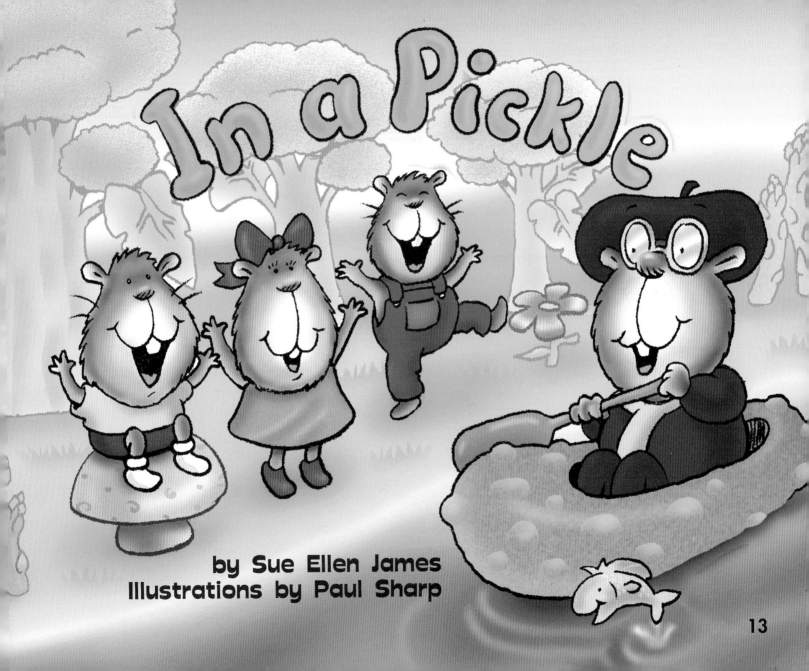

In a Pickle

by Sue Ellen James
Illustrations by Paul Sharp

I am sitting in the middle of the pond. I lost my paddle!

What's that? I see candles. My
friends call, "Paddle over here!"

I have to paddle with this little stick. Too bad. Sniffle, sniffle.

Tickle, tickle. Giggle, giggle.
This is a bit of a tangle!

Then we settle down. We nibble
a little snack.

I have a riddle. I ask with a giggle,
"How do apples fit in a bottle?"

"Here you are—apples in a bottle!"

20

Time for Art!

by Bruce L. Roberts

Illustrations by Sheila Lucas

"It's time for art class," Miss Clark said.
"What do you plan to paint?"

"Help," said Glenn.
"What can I paint? A car?
A plant? A sled? A park?"

"Start with one small mark," said Miss Clark. "Then see what happens."

Carl painted a black shark.
Barb's farm had a big barn
and a red cart.

Dogs bark and flags fly as Kim's band marches by. Arf! Clang! Thud! Clap!

Glenn started with one small
mark. He ended up with stars.
Sparkle! Flash!

Part of art is doing. Part of art is looking. All of art is fun!

YAKS AND YAMS

by Alan Briggs
Illustrations by Michelle Berg

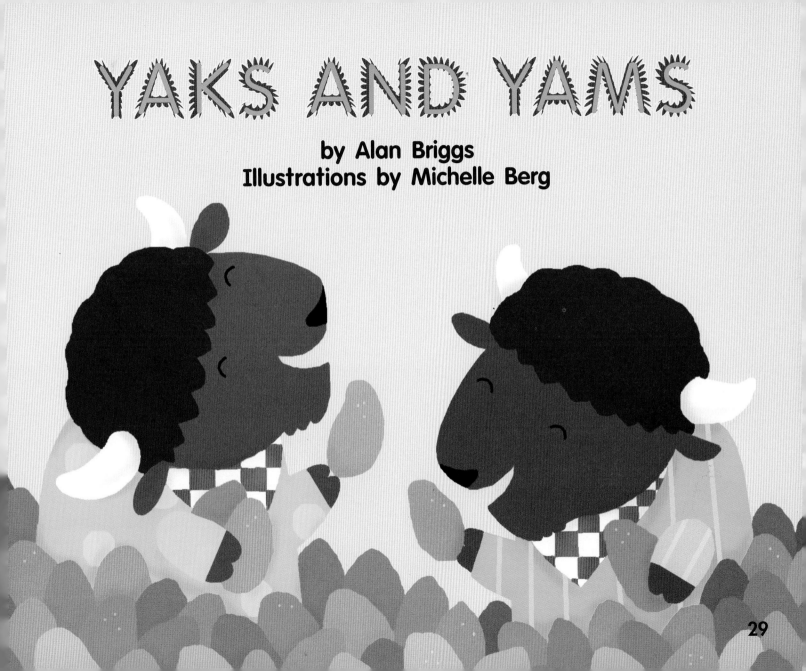

Two little yaks gobble up yams.
Mmm! Mmm! Yum, yum, yams!

"Yams are the best!
Yes, they are! Yams are the
best, the best by far!"

Oh, no! There are no yams left—
no more big, sweet, yams!

No yams are in the yard.
No yams are in the garden.

The two little yaks yip and yelp,
"There are no more yams."

"Stop!" says Gram as
she yanks on some yarn.
"Come with me now!"

"Thanks, Gram! We are all set!
Yams are the best, the best
snack yet!"

York Yak's Yam Stand

CHUCK GETS STUCK

by Linda Clifford

Illustrations by Ruth J. Flanigan

Chuck dug up a home. He lugged
his stuff. Thud, bump, clunk!

"I must have lunch," said Chuck with a grunt—but he made too much!

Yum, yum. Munch, crunch. Chuck didn't stop until he was stuffed!

When Chuck wanted to go back out,
he couldn't! All of a sudden,
he got stuck!

Little Gus Bug was sitting in the sun.
"Help!" said Chuck. "This isn't fun!"

Gus got a bunch of bugs to help.
They tugged and tugged until
Chuck was out.

"Thanks!" cried Chuck. "Thanks so much! Come on. Let's have some lunch!"

Puzzles:

A Hidden
Animal Quiz

by Angela James

Illustrations by
Julia Gorton

Look for me on a farm.
I don't cluck, bark, or honk.
I just quack! Quack!

Look for me in a jungle.
I wiggle and jiggle in the
grass. Hiss! Hisssss!

Look for me at a pond.
I jump far. I'm always quick.
Plop! Do you see me?

I'm at the pond, too. I'm
not quick, but I don't quit!
Look for me in my shell.

I'm in the forest. I take off
like a jet! I zigzag through
the grass. Hop, hop!

I'm in the forest, too.
I have long, sharp quills.
Zing! Don't get jabbed!

Six of us are in the
garden. We zip here and
there. Buzz, buzz, buzz!

Alvin's Home

by Susan DeStefano
Illustrations by Stella Ormai

One morning, Vic Fox was sick.
Off Vic went to visit Alvin the vet.

Alvin, the vet, had lost his home.
"Your tree!" cried Vic. "It fell down!"

More friends found out about Alvin.
"We must help him," said Vic.

Roz Rabbit said, "Look at that old stump. Could Alvin live there?"

"Yes!" cried Vic. "Let's fix up the stump!"
Every animal pitched in to help.

They rubbed and polished and painted.
The stump looked good.

"You're such good friends!" said Alvin.
"You've made me very happy!"

Burt Bird
and His
Friends

by Susan DeStefano

Illustrations
by Casey Craig

I am Burt Bird. I perch
and chirp. I fly all about
looking for things to eat.

All birds must eat a lot.
Sometimes I eat so much
I think I'll just burst!

This is my
friend Gert Turtle.
Her shell is her home.
Hello, Gert! Come out!

A turtle's shell is a very good
home. It's very hard.
Not much can
hurt Gert!

Let's turn by this plant.
This is my friend Kirk.
He's curled up in the dirt.

Kirk lives in the dirt. He even eats dirt! Kirk digs in and stirs things up.

Kirk, Gert, and I all see this
garden in a different way.

OAT MUFFINS

by William Henry

Illustrations by Alexi Natchev

Two little goats trot down the
road. "Sniff, sniff! Muffins!"

"Oh, no!" Toad moans and
groans. "The goats will eat
all my muffins!"

Toad gets a bowl. She shows
the goats how to make their
own oat muffins.

"Have fun, fellows!" Toad
croaks as the goats go home.
"Do not forget the oats."

The goats dump the oats
into a bowl. They mix in
other stuff, too.

       Soap!
       Toast!
       Coal!
       An old coat!
They stir the stuff faster
and faster!

"Our muffins are so good!"
boast the goats. "They are
the sweetest of all!"